Let's Learn
at the
Fire Station!

A Fire Station Field Trip
Becomes a Developmentally Appropriate Thematic Unit
for Your Early Childhood Classroom

Written by Anita Reith Stohs

Illustrated by Becky J. Radtke

This book is dedicated to the Shawnee, KS Fire Department with appreciation for providing information used in the preparation of this book.

This book was packaged for American Teaching Aids by Good Neighbor Press, Inc., Grand Junction, CO.

American Teaching Aids • Minneapolis, MN

Editorial Director: Douglas Rife
Editor: Christopher Hartman
Cover Illustration/Design: Anastasia Mitchell

ATA 2821 Let's Learn at the Fire Station!
ISBN 0-382-29904-3

Table of Contents

Note to the Teacher

A visit to the fire station offers a first-hand opportunity for children to find out the different ways in which the fire fighters prepare for fires and respond to calls for help to put them out. It also gives children a chance to meet fire fighters and learn not to be afraid of them when they are dressed in their fire-fighting gear. Most importantly, the visit alerts children to the real dangers of fires and provides them with information on fire prevention and safety.

At the end of the unit of study described in this book, the student will be able to:

- identify and explain the function of different parts of a fire station
- identify and explain the function of different forms of fire-fighting transportation and equipment
- describe the different kinds of jobs of a fire fighter
- develop strategies for personal safety and fire prevention
- appreciate the work of the fire fighter in seeking to make the children's community a safer place in which to live

The study of the fire station can involve the whole curriculum. The activities in this book have been designed to give you a jumping-off point in many different areas. Adapt them to your own particular class and community situation.

Some young children are easily alarmed at the danger of fire, with excessive fears resulting in nightmares or panic that could prevent life-saving action at the time of a fire. While knowledge of the potential danger of fire is important, try to avoid describing situations that could cause young children to become excessively fearful. Emphasize that you are providing them with safety strategies that help prevent or minimize the danger that a fire can bring. Present the fire fighters as community friends who are there to help if such a need arises.

For useful educational materials on fire prevention and safety, contact the National Fire Protection Association, Batterymarch Park, Quincy, MA 02269-9101.

ATA 2821 © 1993 American Teaching Aids • Minneapolis, MN • Made in U.S.A.

Fire Station Concept Map

Here are suggestions for some of the ways in which a study of the fire station fits in with different areas of the curriculum. Adapt it to your local situation. Pick out specific activities found in this book and add them to the map; then "brainstorm" additional ideas with your class.

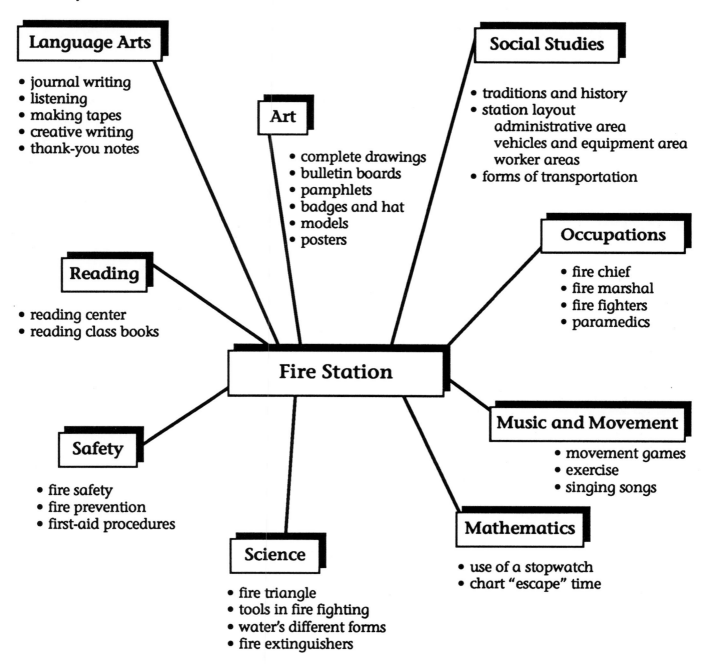

Language Arts
- journal writing
- listening
- making tapes
- creative writing
- thank-you notes

Art
- complete drawings
- bulletin boards
- pamphlets
- badges and hat
- models
- posters

Social Studies
- traditions and history
- station layout
  administrative area
  vehicles and equipment area
  worker areas
- forms of transportation

Reading
- reading center
- reading class books

Occupations
- fire chief
- fire marshal
- fire fighters
- paramedics

Fire Station

Safety
- fire safety
- fire prevention
- first-aid procedures

Music and Movement
- movement games
- exercise
- singing songs

Science
- fire triangle
- tools in fire fighting
- water's different forms
- fire extinguishers

Mathematics
- use of a stopwatch
- chart "escape" time

ATA 2821 © 1993 American Teaching Aids • Minneapolis, MN • Made in U.S.A.

Your Concept Map

```
Language Arts
```
```
Art
```
```
Social Studies
```

Fire Station

```
Responsibility Education
```
```
Careers
```
```
Math and Science
```

ATA 2821 © 1993 American Teaching Aids • Minneapolis, MN • Made in U.S.A.

Sample Two-week Thematic Unit

Here is a suggested two week lesson plan. Adapt it to fit your individual situation.

Days 1-6: *What To Expect at the Fire Station*
Choose activities that acquaint the students with the different parts of the fire station, the people who work in it and the equipment kept there. Adapt activities found in this book to your specific situation. Choose interest centers and extender activities that provide introductory information about fire fighters and their work.

Day 1:
Introduce unit concept maps (pp. 5-6) and help children decide what will be studied. Begin the "Fire Fighters to the Rescue" bulletin board (p. 18) and the milk carton fire station (p. 25). Begin name-tag badges (pp. 21-22).

Day 2:
Draw a concept map showing the different kinds of fire fighters employed by your local fire department. Add the fire fighter figures to the model fire station (p. 40). Begin teaching the "I'm a Fire Fighter" song (p. 39). Do the first part of "Spot Becomes a Fire Fighter" (p. 37).

Day 3:
Learn more about different kinds of fire fighters. Talk about how the methods of fire fighting might vary in different parts of the country or world. Do movement relays related to the work of a fire fighter. Study the uniform worn by fire fighters and make the fire hat (p. 24).

Day 4:
Learn different duties of fire fighters during and after a fire. Do activity pages that reflect these different duties. Choose curriculum extenders that allow the children to write and act out the different activities of a fire fighter at a fire.

Day 5:
Introduce the different types of equipment found in a fire station. Talk about the fire engine and what is on it. Begin the milk carton fire engine (p. 26).

Day 6:
Study other kinds of fire-fighting vehicles and equipment. Make the stand-up transportation figures for the model fire station (p. 33). Briefly introduce the parts of the station you will visit. Make fire-station lunch bag (p. 23).

Days 7-10:
Field trip day; follow-up activities that draw on the experience the children had at the station. Since fire safety is usually stressed at the station, review safety strategies.

Day 7: Visit the station.

Day 8: Review the experience the children had at the station. Make a concept map of the station you visited. Choose activities that call for a reaction based upon the visit.

Day 9: Talk about the science of fire and why it is so dangerous. Choose extender activities that reflect this. Review personal safety. Begin fire safety bulletin board (p. 19).

Day 10: Learn about ways to prevent fires in the home. Complete the activity sheets and send home the one in which parents participate (pp. 41-45). Play fire safety game (p. 46). Finish up with junior volunteer fire-fighter sheet (p. 47).

ATA 2821 © 1993 American Teaching Aids • Minneapolis, MN • Made in U.S.A.

Curriculum Extenders

My Friend, the Fire Fighter *(Art)*
Have children paint a class mural on a large piece of paper showing different ways fire fighters help children. Pictures from the newspapers and magazines may be added to the mural, too.

Fire Safety Poster *(Art)*
Have children tear colored tissue into pieces to represent flames and glue them to a piece of poster board with a mixture of white glue and water. Show children how to draw a "danger" symbol (p. 43) and have them draw danger symbols in the center of their posters. Children can add pictures of fire-causing objects around it. Or, they can make posters showing fire safety guidelines such as "Stop, drop, and roll."

Fire Color Mixing *(Art)*
Explore different colors seen in a fire. Put yellow, red and blue finger paint in a zip-lock bag. Tape the end securely. Have the children squeeze the three colors together to see what happens when they are mixed.

First Aid Center *(First Aid)*
Set up a "first aid center" with play medical equipment and dolls for patients. Supply white shirts for uniforms. Let the children pretend to be medics helping people in an emergency.

First Aid Techniques *(First Aid)*
Have someone from the Red Cross or a school nurse come in to teach simple first aid techniques to children, especially in the care of burns and smoke inhalation.

Newspaper Center *(Language Arts)*
Provide paper and pencils. Let the children pretend to be newspaper reporters writing up reports of how fire fighters put out a fire. Have them write the reports on long strips of paper to be pasted onto a piece of poster board with the name of your local newspaper on top. They can include drawings or photographs that illustrate their article.

Fire Station Book *(Language Arts)*
Cut out several pages in the shape of the fire station. Have the children write the story of their visit to the fire station inside the pages.

ATA 2821 © 1993 American Teaching Aids • Minneapolis, MN • Made in U.S.A.

Curriculum Extenders

Tape Center *(Language Arts)*
Put out a tape player and blank tape. Let children tape pretend fire station telephone and radio conversations. One option could be a tape of the sounds they might hear as the fire is being put out.

Big Book *(Language Arts)*
After the visit to the fire station, talk about the experience with the children. Have them help you write a story about it. Put the words on large pieces of poster board. Let small groups of children illustrate the individual pages. Put them together for a big book to read to the class. When finished, add the book to the reading center.

The Day I Was a... *(Language Arts)*
Ask the children to pretend that they are fire fighters for a day. What kind of fire fighter would they like to be? What would they do? Ask them to write a story about what their day would be like, then draw themselves as fire fighters. As an option, children can write the story in a shape book cut out like a fire fighter.

Thank-you Notes *(Language Arts)*
Using a badge pattern as a guide, fold pieces of paper and cut badge-shaped cards. Have the children write and illustrate their own thank-you notes to the officers who showed them through the fire station.

Time To Escape *(Mathematics)*
Use a stopwatch to time escape times through a tunnel, or out of a room or building. Chart the times. Or chart how fast it takes to get on boots and a raincoat.

Exercise Time *(Movement)*
It's exercise time for the fire fighters at the station.
Have your class exercise to music.

Escape Route Practice *(Movement)*
Cover a long table or several desks with a blanket and have the children practice crawling under smoke to a door at the other end. When they get there, show how they would check to see if the door handle was hot, and, if so, show how they would crawl to a pretend window to get out. Or, set up two "tunnels" and have a relay crawling through it.

ATA 2821 © 1993 American Teaching Aids • Minneapolis, MN • Made in U.S.A.

Curriculum Extenders

What's My Fire-Fighting Job? *(Movement)*
Have one child act out movements for a specific kind of fire-fighting job. Give the class three guesses to tell what the job is. The person who guesses the right answer gets to be the next one to act out a job. If no one guesses the right answer, the child who is "it" chooses a new person to take his place.

Cup Brigade *(Movement and Social Studies)*
Years ago fires were fought by bucket brigades. Go outside and have a "cup" brigade. Give each child a paper cup. Divide into two or more teams. Start each side with a full cup. Have each child pass the water to the next child until they get to the end. The side with the fullest cup at the end is the winner.

Fire-Horse Relay *(Movement and Social Studies)*
Early fire engines were pulled by horses. Go outside and divide into two teams. Have the two teams split into two sections, and have each side pull a bucket of water in a wagon back and forth. See which team has the most water at the end. As an indoor activity, omit the bucket of water and see which team is the fastest.

Book Center *(Reading)*
Check out books from school and public libraries about the work of a fire fighter, fire prevention, and personal fire safety. Put out the books for children to read. Include any class books on fire fighting written during the unit. Encourage the children to write or give oral reports on the books.

Fire Safety Center *(Reading and Language Arts)*
Obtain pamphlets on fire prevention and safety from your local fire station. Let the children look at them. Provide strips of paper for the children and ask them to write their own pamphlets. Put the student pamphlets out with the other ones.

What Does Fire Need To Burn? *(Science)*
Draw a triangle on the board and write the words "heat," "oxygen," and "fuel" on the ends. Call it the "fire triangle." Talk about how a fire needs all three of these to burn. Explain that all a fireman can normally remove are heat and oxygen. Depending on the age of your class, do simple experiments to show the need for all three. Discuss what elements are present to cause a fire to burn and the methods of extinguishing a fire. Explain why water doesn't work sometimes and carbon dioxide must be used. Tell how fog and foam are used to put out such fires.

ATA 2821 © 1993 American Teaching Aids • Minneapolis, MN • Made in U.S.A.

Curriculum Extenders

Fire Extinguishers and How They Work *(Science)*
Find out what chemicals are present in a fire extinguisher.
Explain to children the chemical reaction that takes place as it is
used to put a fire out.

Different States of Matter *(Science)*
Explain how matter is solid, liquid, or gas. Talk about how all three
forms of water can be present at a fire in winter.

Water Pump *(Science)*
Put water in a container and provide toy pumps. Have the
children experiment with pumping water and talk about how the
pump works.

Water Play *(Science)*
Supply dippers, sieves and other containers with and without holes.
Have the children experiment to find out what holds water and
what does not. Talk about different ways the fire department carries
water to the fire.

Fire Fighters at Work *(Social Studies)*
Gather together models of fire engines and trucks. Have children
color in boxes to make a station and houses. Place them over a
large piece of paper or cardboard and let the children draw roads for
the fire vehicles. Let the children act out fire fighters going to a fire.

Equipment Center *(Social Studies)*
Put together an interest center with various types of equipment
used by a fire fighter. Options include a hat, raincoat, and a short
piece of hose. Let the children pretend they are fire fighters using
the equipment.

Fire Fighting in Different Places *(Social Studies)*
Talk about the different kinds of fires found in various parts of our
country. Find out the special ways fires need to be fought in
different climates.

Fire-Fighting Traditions *(Social Studies)*
Fire fighters are big on "tradition." Talk about how traditions
show history. Ask a fire fighter to tell you about traditions of fire
fighters in general and in the station you visit.

History of Fire Fighting *(Social Studies)*
Prepare a class book about the history of fire fighting.

The History of Fire Fighting

ATA 2821 © 1993 American Teaching Aids • Minneapolis, MN • Made in U.S.A.

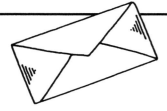

Letters and Forms

Date_____

Dear Parents,

On _____ our class is planning a field trip to the _____ Fire Station. During the coming weeks, we will be doing a variety of class projects designed to help us prepare for and expand upon what the children will see and hear on this visit.

A visit to a fire station provides a way to help children learn firsthand about how fire fighters seek to make the children's community a safer place in which to live. The children will learn what is found in a fire station, what its workers do, and what they use to do their job. In addition, the students will learn strategies for personal safety and fire prevention.

We will be needing volunteers to drive students to the fire station and back, and to help with the visit. We will leave at _____ and plan to be back at _____. If you can help, please indicate this on the permission slip found on the bottom of the page.

Please send a sack lunch with your child on the day of the field trip. Complete the following permission slip and return to me by _____.

Thank you,

_____

Permission Slip

_____ Yes, my child, _____, has permission to go to the _____ Fire Station on _____, 19_____.

_____ I will be happy to drive students to the station and help supervise them there. My car has seatbelts for _____ students.

Signed:_____ Date: _____

Home phone: _____ Work phone: _____

ATA 2821 © 1993 American Teaching Aids • Minneapolis, MN • Made in U.S.A.

Countdown Checklist

Use this checklist to help get ready for the big day of the fire station field trip.

Begin Countdown:

_____ Arrange the date for the field trip with the fire department.

_____ Follow school procedure for setting up the date for the field trip and obtaining permission for the trip.

_____ Order school buses or parent drivers for the trip.

_____ Decide whether you plan on taking a sack lunch on your trip. If so, notify the school cafeteria.

_____ Visit the fire department yourself to work out specific arrangements for the trip. See what parts of the building the students will be touring. Pick up brochures for use with classroom activities.

_____ Consider lining up publicity for your trip with a local newspaper or TV station.

_____ Check out books from school and public libraries.

_____ Determine what bulletin boards and art activities you will make and gather art supplies.

_____ Decide what forms and activity sheets you will use and make copies accordingly.

_____ _____

_____ _____

_____ _____

_____ _____

_____ _____

_____ _____

Countdown Checklist

The Countdown Continues:

_____ Send out parent letter with permission slips.

_____ See that all slips are collected.

_____ Determine specific helping duties for adult volunteers.

_____ Reconfirm date and time with adult volunteers. Let them know specifics of helping duties.

_____ Develop a field trip itinerary for your departure, arrival, and return. Allow for bathroom breaks. Duplicate copies for adult helpers.

_____ If you are taking a sack lunch, decide where and when you will wash up before lunch and where lunch will be eaten.

_____ Make arrangements for photography or videotaping for the field trip.

_____ Double check on arrangements with the fire department.

_____ Double check on arrangements with the bus company.

_____ There usually is a first-aid kit on the bus and first-aid equipment at the fire station. Decide what first-aid supplies you need to carry yourself. Keep in mind special medical needs of the class.

_____ Prepare thank-you notes to send after the trip.

_____ Locate coolers or carry-on boxes for lunches.

_____ Locate a backpack or tote bag for carrying special supplies.

_____ Plan activities for bus or car ride, i.e. songs, games, pencil and paper activities, seating chart, passenger lists, and buddies.

_____ Complete badges and sack projects.

_____ Deal with possible anxieties about the trip.

_____ Practice appropriate behavior for the trip, i.e., how to ask questions, how to shake hands, and how to say thank you. Encourage role-playing activities.

_____ _____

_____ _____

_____ _____

Junior Fire Fighter Guidelines

Go over these guidelines with the students before the field trip. If your students can write, enlist their help transferring these suggestions onto posterboard before your trip. Use the badge patterns on pages 21 and 22 to make an attractive border for each poster.

On the way:
1. Stay in your seat and use the seat belt.
2. Keep your hands and possessions to yourself.
3. Watch the noise level (talk quietly, without shouting).
4. Thank the driver and helpers at the end of the trip.

At the station:
1. Talk quietly, and then only where permitted.
2. Keep still while your guide is talking to you.
3. Listen to what the guide has to say. Raise your hand if you have questions.
4. Stay with your partner as you move from one area to another.
5. Water may be on the floor in the fire engine room. Do not run or you could slip and fall. You could also be hurt by falling onto equipment.
6. Equipment needs to be ready for a fire. Do not touch it unless you have permission.
7. Follow any special instructions given by your guide.
8. Take turns looking at or trying out any equipment shown to the class.
9. Thank the guide and any other helpful people in the fire station.

Other guidelines to follow:

_____

_____

_____

_____

_____

ATA 2821 © 1993 American Teaching Aids • Minneapolis, MN • Made in U.S.A.

Teacher Debriefing

Fire Station Field Trip   Date _____

Contacts I made for this trip:

Name	Phone Number	Position	Comments

Scheduling: Did I have enough time for planning? When should I start next time?

_____

Was the day of the field trip scheduled appropriately? What should I leave out, or include, the next time I plan this trip?

_____

Pre-trip Activities: What activities worked best? What did I/the students enjoy the most? What should be included or eliminated next time?

_____

Field Trip Day Activities: What was the highlight of the day?

_____

What was the least successful activity?_____

Miscellaneous notes to myself: _____

_____

Good Job, Teacher!

ATA 2821 © 1993 American Teaching Aids • Minneapolis, MN • Made in U.S.A.

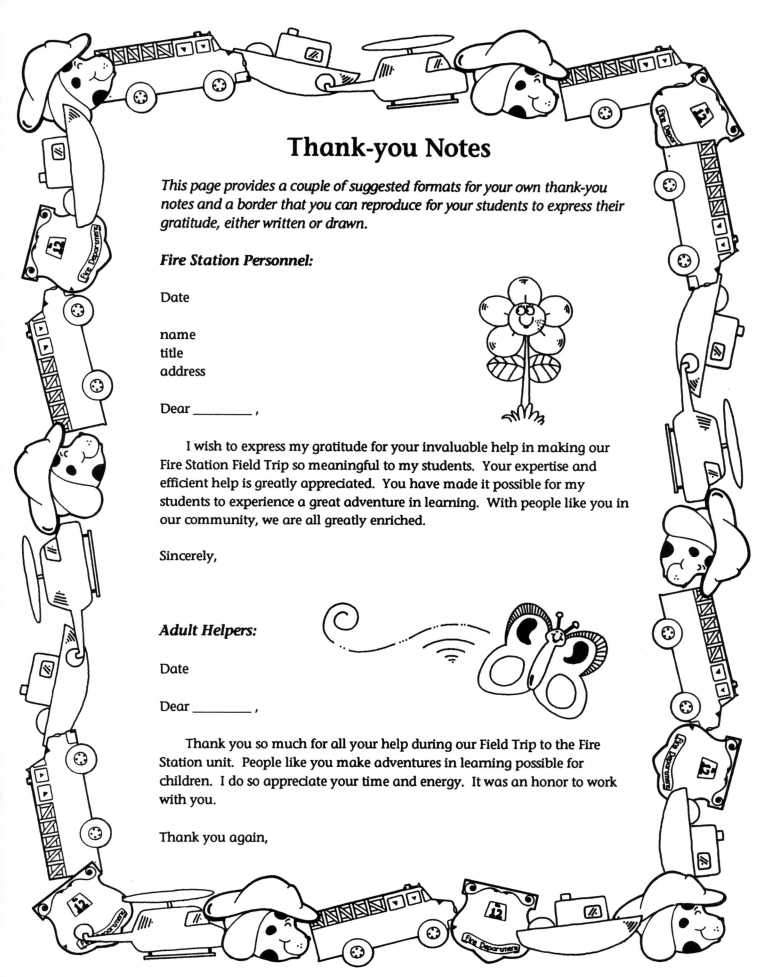

Thank-you Notes

This page provides a couple of suggested formats for your own thank-you notes and a border that you can reproduce for your students to express their gratitude, either written or drawn.

Fire Station Personnel:

Date

name
title
address

Dear _____ ,

    I wish to express my gratitude for your invaluable help in making our Fire Station Field Trip so meaningful to my students. Your expertise and efficient help is greatly appreciated. You have made it possible for my students to experience a great adventure in learning. With people like you in our community, we are all greatly enriched.

Sincerely,

Adult Helpers:

Date

Dear _____ ,

    Thank you so much for all your help during our Field Trip to the Fire Station unit. People like you make adventures in learning possible for children. I do so appreciate your time and energy. It was an honor to work with you.

Thank you again,

"Fire Fighters to the Rescue" Bulletin Board

Create a bulletin board illustration of a large rectangular house with a triangular roof. Draw windows and a door. Add a few flames to the roof.

Have the children help make a class bulletin board showing different kinds of fire fighters. Put the names of different kinds of fire fighters in a bag and have the children draw them. Provide books that show these fire fighters in action. Give the children equal rectangles of paper. Have the children draw, color or paint a picture of their assigned fire fighter, then cut it out and attach it to the bulletin board around and on the burning house.

Option: To avoid frightening the sensitive children in the class, change the burning house to the local fire station and have the children put the fire figures around it. Add the picture of Captain Spot, found in this book, and the words "Captain Spot and His Friends."

Captain Spot and His Friends

ATA 2821 © 1993 American Teaching Aids • Minneapolis, MN • Made in U.S.A.

"Do's and Don'ts of Fire Safety" Bulletin Board

Write at the top of the bulletin board: "Captain Spot Says"

Below this write "Do" and "Don't," with a line between them. Give the children circles. Have them draw pictures to illustrate fire safety or danger. If danger, have them draw a "warning line" across the circle. Put the "do's" on one side and the "don'ts" on the other. Duplicate the picture of Captain Spot, found on the next page, and add it to the picture.

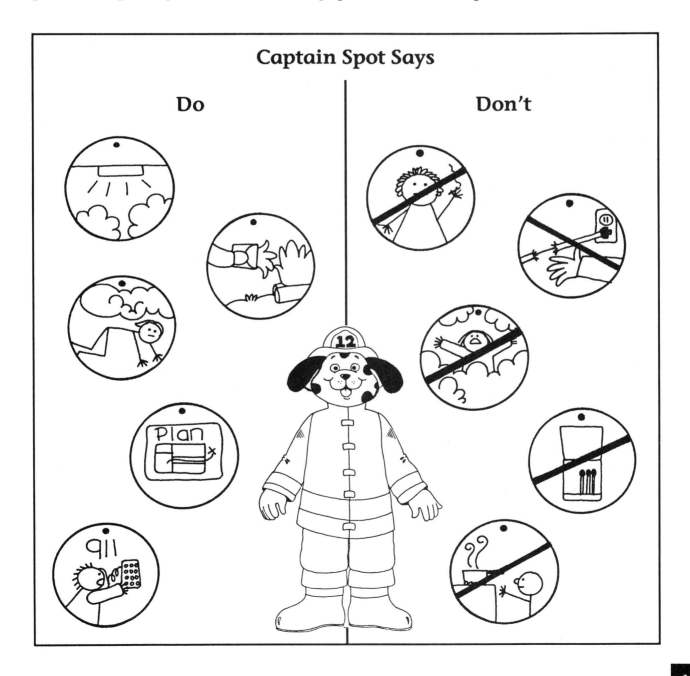

ATA 2821 © 1993 American Teaching Aids • Minneapolis, MN • Made in U.S.A.

Captain Spot

Color the picture of Captain Spot. Draw and color the equipment he needs to do his job.

ATA 2821 © 1993 American Teaching Aids • Minneapolis, MN • Made in U.S.A.

Badges

Badges can be used for easy identification of your students on the day of the field trip. Divide the class into groups that provide the most meaningful learning experience for each student. Make sure that the shy student has a buddy. Try to separate those children who tend to distract each other easily. Mix boys and girls. Try to keep groups under eight; more than that decreases the effectiveness of your fire station guide. Remember to make badges for the adult helpers, too! As an alternative to writing individual names on the badges, use your school name. Duplicate these forms on brightly-colored paper and laminate them after the students have decorated them. You will need: badge outline for each student and adult, colored markers, scissors, brightly colored yarn and a hole punch.

CAPTAIN SPOT

Another Way To Use These Patterns: Enlarge the patterns on your copier and ask your students to color them. Use them for a colorful border for a doorway or bulletin board.

ATA 2821 © 1993 American Teaching Aids • Minneapolis, MN • Made in U.S.A.

Badges

BADGE

No.
12

_____
Name

Fire Department

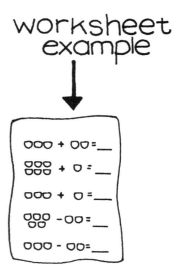

worksheet example

Another Way To Use These Patterns: Reduce the pattern of your choice and design your own worksheet for math problems. *(see above.)*

AERIAL TRUCK

Name

ATA 2821 © 1993 American Teaching Aids • Minneapolis, MN • Made in U.S.A.

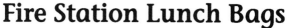

Fire Station Lunch Bags

Materials
Paper bag
Glue
Crayons

Directions
1. Color and cut out the picture of the fire station found on this page.
2. Write in the name of the fire station you will visit.
3. Draw fire trucks inside the door. Add fire fighters, too.
4. Glue the picture to the front of the paper bag.
5. Draw windows on the other sides of the bag. Draw fire fighters looking out of the windows.
6. Color in the rest of the truck on the other side of the paper bag.

_____ Fire Station

example

ATA 2821 © 1993 American Teaching Aids • Minneapolis, MN • Made in U.S.A.

My Fire Hat

Find out what color hat your community's fire fighters wear. Use crayons or paint to color, then cut out the front of the fire hat found on the bottom of this page. Glue it to the center of a paper plate. Color the rest of the paper plate. Cut out the top outline of the hat. Fold up the top of the hat and wear it.

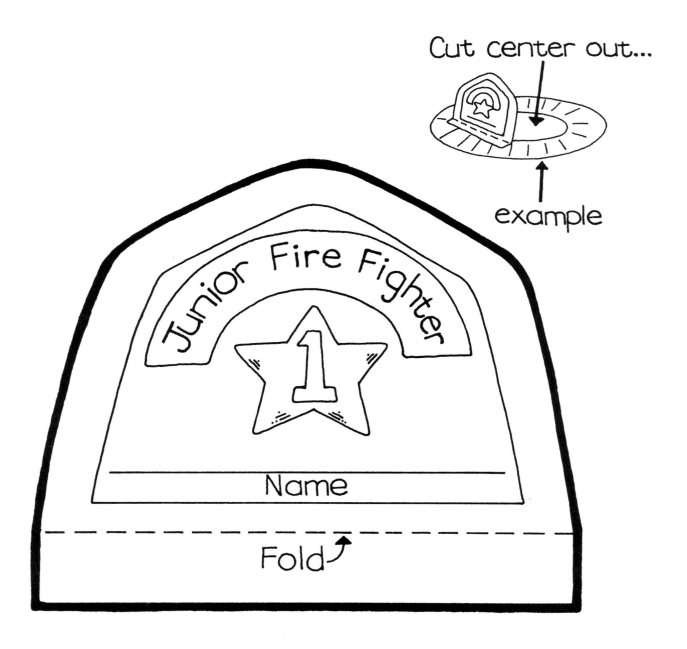

Cut center out...

example

Junior Fire Fighter

1

Name

Fold

ATA 2821 © 1993 American Teaching Aids • Minneapolis, MN • Made in U.S.A.

Milk Carton Fire Station

Materials
- empty half-gallon milk carton
- construction paper
- cardboard
- glue
- markers or crayons
- scissors

Teacher Preparation
Cut the bottom from each milk carton; then cut two slits on the bottom of one side for a fold-up door. Cut pieces of construction paper that will cover all 4 sides of each milk carton. After these have been glued to the milk cartons, your students can cut the paper along the existing cuts in the carton to form the fold-up door.

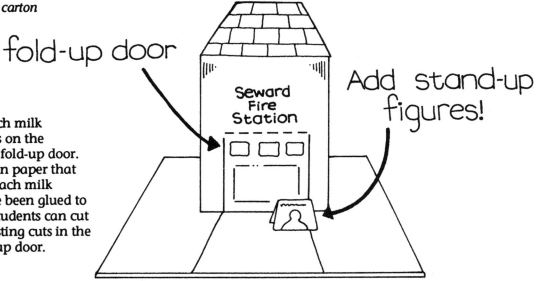

fold-up door

Seward Fire Station

Add stand-up figures!

Directions

1. Draw shingles onto the roof and glue the roof to the top of the carton.

2. Draw a door over the fold-up door of your milk carton. Write the name of your local fire station above the door.

3. Cut around the door on two sides so it will fold up.

4. Draw windows on the other sides of the station.

5. Cut cardboard into a square base for your station.

6. Cut construction paper to fit onto the square. Use green for grass and gray for the road in front of the station.

7. Add stand-up figures of fire fighters and their vehicles as they are studied. Use the figures to make up stories about your fire fighters' station. Write the stories down.

8. As an option, also make a milk carton house. Cut construction paper flames that can fit into slits cut into the house. Remove the flames when your fire fighters "come and put the fire out."

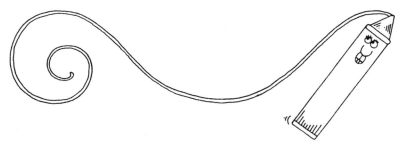

ATA 2821 © 1993 American Teaching Aids • Minneapolis, MN • Made in U.S.A.

Milk Carton Fire Engine

Materials
- empty milk carton
- egg-carton cup
- tempera paint
- paint brushes
- two empty paper towel tubes
- construction paper
- markers or crayons
- yarn
- tape, glue, scissors

Teacher Preparation
- Cut out one side (the side that will be the bottom of the fire engine) and the top of each milk carton. Then cut the half-circles out along the bottom where the cardboard tube wheels will be glued.

- Cut two cardboard tubes 1" to 1½" longer than the bottom of each carton.

- Cut one egg cup for each project from egg cartons.

- Trace and cut construction paper for the front, sides and top of the fire engines. The students can glue the paper to the carton.

Directions
1. Trace construction paper to fit the sides and top of the fire engine and glue the paper to the carton.

2. Use a marker or crayon to decorate the engine to look like one used by your local fire department. Draw Captain Spot driving the fire engine. As an option, use construction paper for details.

3. Paint each tube black; when dry, fit under the fire engine for wheels.

4. Paint the egg-carton cup red; when dry, glue it to the top of the engine.

5. Cut a piece of yarn for a hose. Tape one end to the fire engine and wrap tape around the other end of the yarn for a nozzle.

6. Use your fire engine to act out stories about fire fighters. Write down the stories.

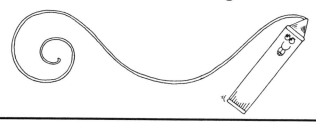

ATA 2821 © 1993 American Teaching Aids • Minneapolis, MN • Made in U.S.A.

Ask a Fire Fighter

What would you like to know about the jobs of a fire fighter? Write down your question. When you are visiting the station, ask the fire fighter your question. After the field trip, write down the answer to your question.

Question: _____

_____

_____

_____

Answer: _____

_____

_____

_____

Draw a picture that shows the answer to your question.

ATA 2821 © 1993 American Teaching Aids • Minneapolis, MN • Made in U.S.A.

Our Trip to the Fire Station

by

_____

To the Teacher: Copy this page for your students to write a descriptive paragraph or poem about their experience at the Fire Station.

ATA 2821 © 1993 American Teaching Aids • Minneapolis, MN • Made in U.S.A.

Ready for the Fire

Captain Spot is ready to go to the fire. He wears clothes that protect him when he works. Connect the dashed lines to see his outfit. Find out what color clothes a fire fighter in your fire department wears. Color Captain Spot with the same colors.

Helmet

Turn-out Coat

Gloves

Turn-out Pants

Steel-toed Boots

ATA 2821 © 1993 American Teaching Aids • Minneapolis, MN • Made in U.S.A.

Ways To Get to a Fire

What does each kind of fire vehicle do? Follow the fire hoses to find out.

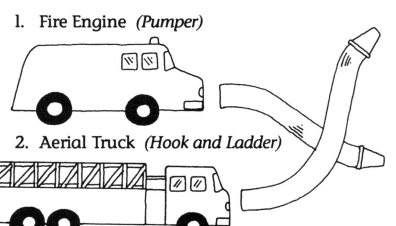

1. Fire Engine *(Pumper)*

2. Aerial Truck *(Hook and Ladder)*

3. Support Vehicle

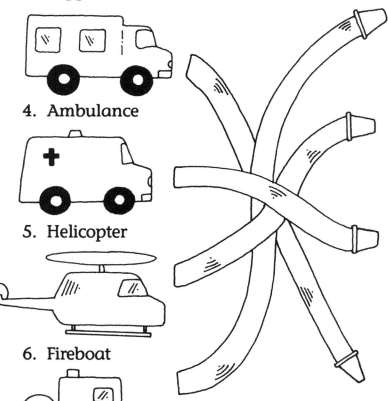

4. Ambulance

5. Helicopter

6. Fireboat

A long truck with ladders that can go up a high building.

Carries hoses to the fire where fire fighters will hook them up to a fire hydrant.

Pumps water out of the river, ocean, or lake to fight fires on boats, docks or buildings near bodies of water.

Carries forest-fire fighters and supplies where fire trucks cannot go.

Carries paramedics and their first-aid supplies.

Carries supplies to help fire fighters at the fire. Can carry special chemicals, a vacuum to clean up water, material to patch roofs, and refills of fresh air for the fire fighters.

ATA 2821 © 1993 American Teaching Aids • Minneapolis, MN • Made in U.S.A.

First at the Fire: The Fire Engine

The fire engine is a hose truck. Also known as a pumper, it arrives at a fire first. It squirts water from the fire hydrant to fight the fire so fire fighters can go into the burning building. It also has extra water in its tank.

Color in the parts of the new fire engine at Captain Spot's fire station.

1. Driver's Seat

2. Jump Seat

3. Tools

4. Pump Panel

5. Hose Bed

6. Water Tank

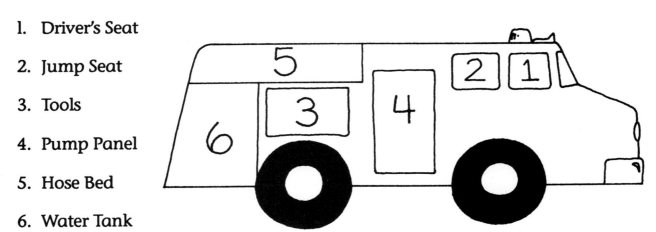

What is different about the fire engine at your fire station? Finish the drawing below to look like the engine at your fire station.

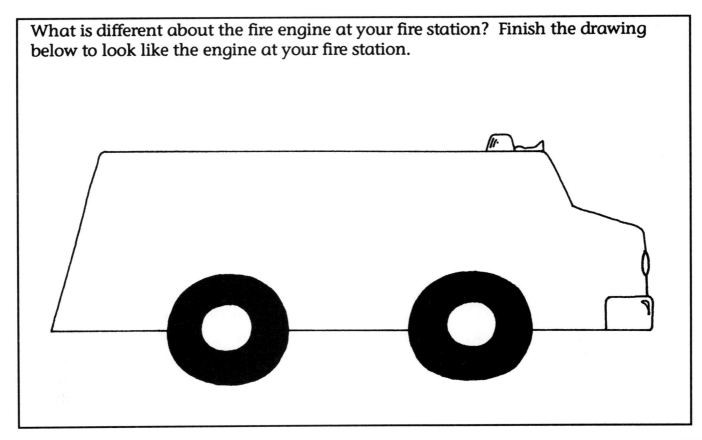

ATA 2821 © 1993 American Teaching Aids • Minneapolis, MN • Made in U.S.A.

Tools on the Truck

On the fire engine are some of the same tools you might see at home. After a fire, the driver of the fire engine has to make sure that all the tools are put back on the truck. Help Fire Fighter Dot put her tools back on the truck. Connect the dashed lines on the tools and glue the correct name under each tool.

Talk about how these tools help with a fire. (Hint: The broom is used for grass fires.)

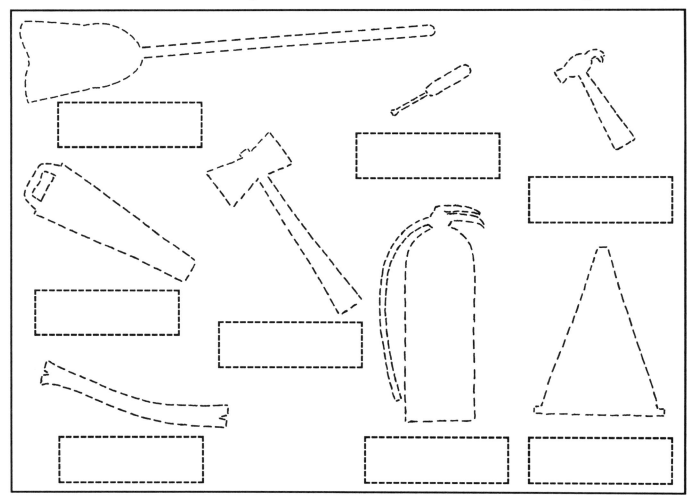

Cut out the tool names below and glue them where they belong.

| axe | screwdriver | safety cone | fire extinguisher |
| crowbar | saw | broom | hammer |

ATA 2821 © 1993 American Teaching Aids • Minneapolis, MN • Made in U.S.A.

Off to the Fire: Stand-up Transportation Figures

Talk about how these different kinds of fire-fighting vehicles are used in fire emergencies. Finish the pictures and color them, then fold them on their dashed lines to stand them up. Add them to your milk carton fire station. Make up your own stand-up engines and trucks like those used to fight fires in your community.

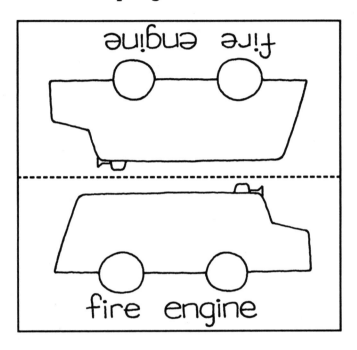

fire engine

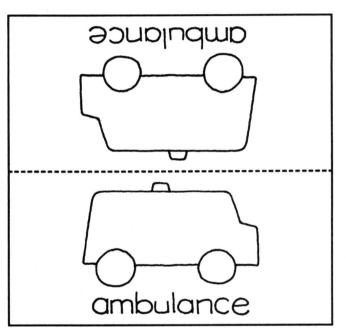

ambulance

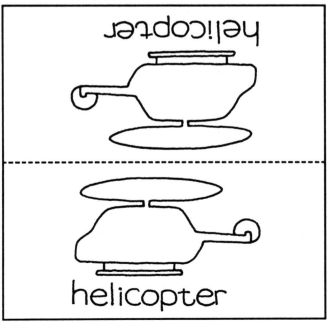

helicopter

fireboat

ATA 2821 © 1993 American Teaching Aids • Minneapolis, MN • Made in U.S.A.

At the Fire

Different people do different jobs at the fire. Listen as your teacher reads about fire fighters' jobs.

Dan Baker works the pump panel of his fire engine.

Sandy Petersen fastens the hose to the hydrant.

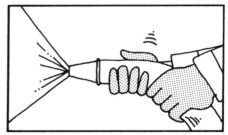

Aaron Blumenthal squirts water from the hose onto the fire.

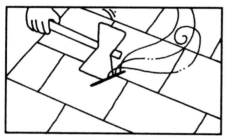

Al Weilborg uses an axe to cut a hole in the roof to let out steam and heat.

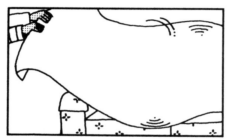

Theresa Garcia covers furniture with a tarp to keep it dry.

Patrick Kelly climbs a ladder to fight a fire in a high building.

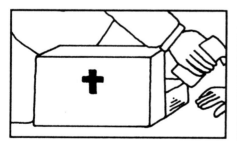

Anthony Salata gives first aid to people injured at the fire.

Kenya Phillips checks fire fighters to make sure they are not getting sick from the heat and the smoke.

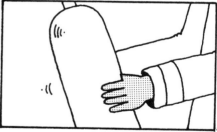

Ming Lee gives new fresh air tanks to fire fighters.

What kind of fire fighting job would you like to do at a fire? Finish the sentence:

I would like to_____ because _____

_____

Turn the sheet over and draw a picture of yourself as a fire fighter.

ATA 2821 © 1993 American Teaching Aids • Minneapolis, MN • Made in U.S.A.

Volunteers on the Way

Only three fire fighters are on duty at Captain Spot's fire station when the alarm goes off. They go on the fire truck first. Other fire fighters hear about the fire on their radios and follow. Draw the other fire fighters, or volunteers, helping at the fire.

Do volunteers help at your fire station? Ask how they know when and where the fire is. Write what you find out here.

_____

_____

_____

_____

_____

_____

_____

ATA 2821 © 1993 American Teaching Aids • Minneapolis, MN • Made in U.S.A.

Going to the Fire

The driver of a fire engine has an important job to do. He needs to know where he is going and how he will get there. He is in charge of the equipment on the truck. He decides when to use it and sees that it is put back in place after the fire is over.

The driver of the fire engine is checking the big map in the firehouse to find the best way to get to the fire. Show him the way he should go.

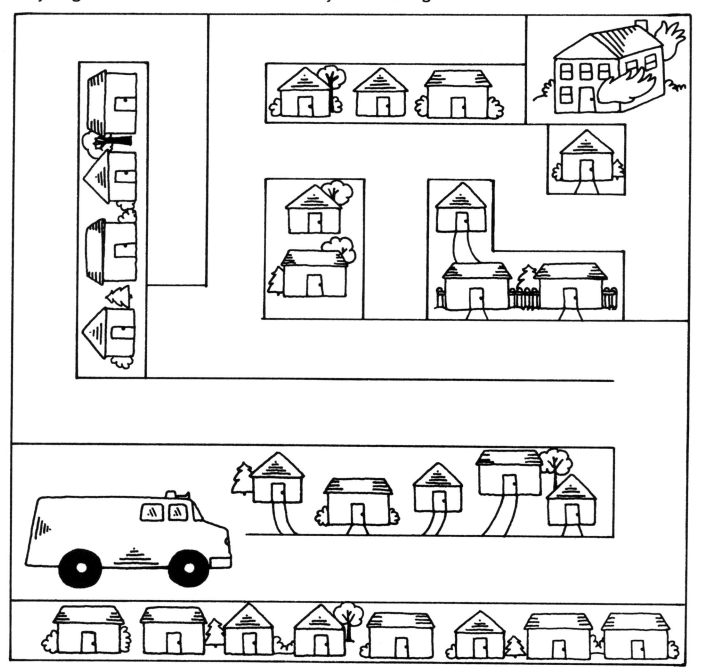

ATA 2821 © 1993 American Teaching Aids • Minneapolis, MN • Made in U.S.A.

Spot Becomes a Fire Fighter

Listen as your teacher reads how Spot became a fire fighter. Ask a fire fighter at your local station to tell how he or she became a fire fighter.

Captain Spot was working at another job when he decided to be a volunteer fire fighter. He took classes and had to pass a written test. He had to pass a physical test, too, to make sure he was healthy. He liked being a fire fighter so much he took some college courses about fire fighting. When there was an opening at the fire station, he applied for the job. Now he is a full-time fire fighter.

Captain Spot says you must be at least eighteen years of age to be a fire fighter. Both men and women can be fire fighters. It is important to know how to use the fire-fighting equipment and machines correctly because people's lives and property depend upon your doing your job well. You need a good education so you can read and understand how to do your job. You need at least a high school education, with some college courses in the area of fire fighting.

Captain Spot says that a fire fighter is someone who enjoys helping other people. The work they do is dangerous, but exciting. The most important thing about being a fire fighter is saving the lives of other people. He hopes that some of you will be fire fighters like him, either as volunteers or paid workers.

Ask the fire fighter who shows you his station on your field trip how and why he became a fire fighter. Write his answers down in the space below:

_____

_____

_____

_____

_____

_____

_____

_____

_____

ATA 2821 © 1993 American Teaching Aids • Minneapolis, MN • Made in U.S.A.

Waiting for a Fire: Fire Fighters on Duty

The fire fighters on duty at the station have a "day room" where they eat, watch TV or study. Here is a fire fighter eating his lunch. What do you think he likes to eat? Draw it on his plate.

At night the fire fighter sleeps with her boots and pants ready to jump into the minute the alarm wakes her up. Draw the tired fire fighter on her bunk.

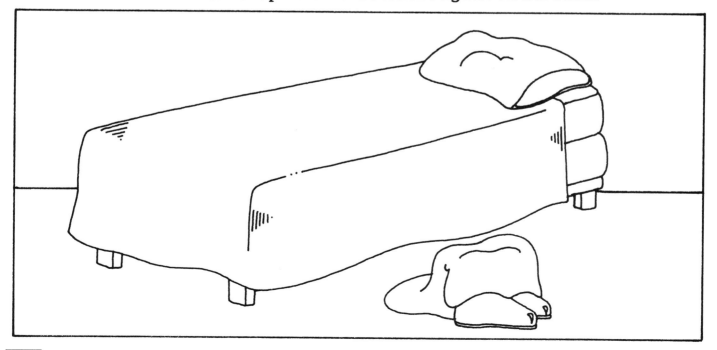

ATA 2821 © 1993 American Teaching Aids • Minneapolis, MN • Made in U.S.A.

"I'm a Fire Fighter" Song

Tune: *Mulberry Bush*

1.   This is the way I pull on my boots, pull on my boots, pull on my boots;
        This is the way I pull on my boots,
        I'm a fire fighter. *(Pretend to pull on boots)*

2.   This is the way I drive the fire truck, drive the fire truck, drive the
        fire truck, etc.
        I'm a fire fighter. *(Pretend to turn wheel)*

3.   This is the way I fasten the hose, fasten the hose, fasten the hose, etc.
        I'm a fire fighter. *(Pretend to attach hose to hydrant)*

4.   This is the way I squirt the water, squirt the water, squirt the water, etc.
        I'm a fire fighter. *(Pretend to hold hose and squirt water)*

5.   This is the way I climb the ladder, climb the ladder, climb the ladder, etc.
        I'm a fire fighter. *(Pretend to climb ladder)*

6.   This is the way I roll up the hose, roll up the hose, roll up the hose, etc.
        I'm a fire fighter. *(Pretend to roll up hose)*

Think up some other fire fighter activities and add them to this song. Write a new verse for the song. Tell what motions go with the words.

Verses: _____

_____

_____

Motions: _____

_____

39

ATA 2821 © 1993 American Teaching Aids • Minneapolis, MN • Made in U.S.A.

Fire Fighters at Work: Stand-up Figures

Talk about how these fire fighters help us. Color in their faces and uniforms. Add a fire fighter like one at the fire station you visit. Fold on dashed lines and add them to your milk carton fire station.

Crawl Low Under Smoke

These children are in the lecture room of the fire station. They are learning how to crawl low under smoke. Smoke is hot and has gases that are dangerous to breathe. It fills the top of the room first. If you have no other way to get out of a fire, crawl several inches from the floor.

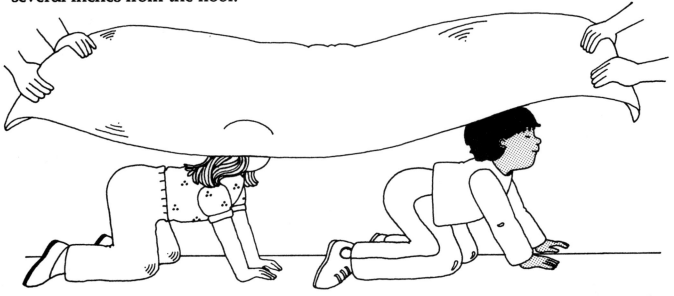

Practice crawling under a table or row of desks so you will know how to get out of a smoky room in case of fire. Draw a picture of how you would crawl low in a fire.

ATA 2821 © 1993 American Teaching Aids • Minneapolis, MN • Made in U.S.A.

Stop, Drop and Roll

These children are practicing what they will do in case their clothes ever catch on fire.

Use the code to fill in the signs, then write the words in the sentences below them.

Code:

⊖ △ □ ✕ Ƨ ∧ ⌢
D L O P R S T

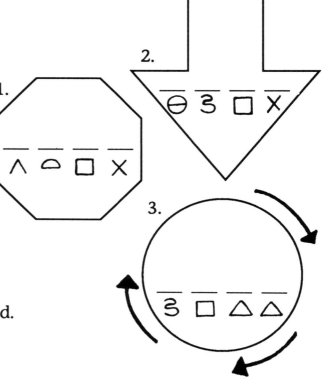

If your clothes catch on fire:

1. ____ ____ ____ ____ , don't run.

2. ____ ____ ____ ____ to the ground.

3. Cover your face with your hands and ____ ____ ____ ____ over and over.

Practice these steps until you can do them easily.

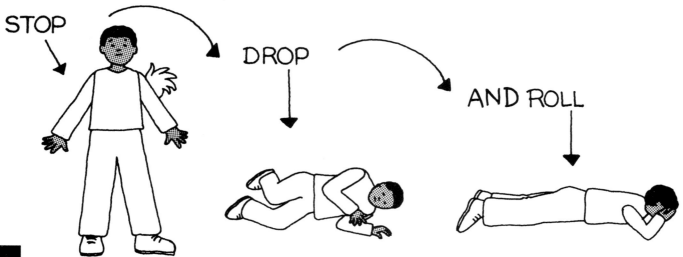

STOP   DROP   AND ROLL

ATA 2821 © 1993 American Teaching Aids • Minneapolis, MN • Made in U.S.A.

Stay Away From Danger!

Draw a danger circle ⊘ (a circle with a line across it) over each of the following things that could burn you.

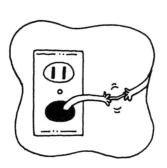

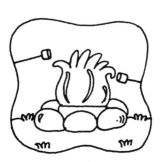

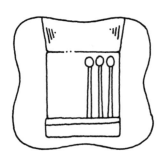

43

ATA 2821 © 1993 American Teaching Aids • Minneapolis, MN • Made in U.S.A.

Safety Watch: What's Wrong With the Picture?

Find ten things that could cause a fire in this picture. Put an *x* on each dangerous thing.

ATA 2821 © 1993 American Teaching Aids • Minneapolis, MN • Made in U.S.A.

Fire Safety in the Home

Take this page home and go through it with an adult.

1. **Escape Plan:** Draw a floor plan of your house. Show two ways of getting out of every room. If you live in an apartment, include the way to leave the building.

2. **Practice Your Escape Plan:** Practice getting out of different parts of the house, especially the bedrooms. *Remember: GET OUT FAST and DON'T GO BACK, NO MATTER WHAT!*

2. **Choose A Meeting Place:** Finish the sentence: In case of a fire, we will meet at

    _____

3. **Calling for Help:** Finish the sentence: In case of a fire, we *(an adult, if possible)* _____ will call for help at a telephone. The number to call is _____. *(Memorize the number.)*

4. **Know How To Unlock All Locks and Open Windows:** Practice how to unlock all locks and doors in your house.

5. **Check Your Smoke Detectors:** Check the following:

    _____ We have a smoke detector in each level of our home, basement included.

    _____ We have a smoke detector outside each sleeping area.

    _____ All detectors have fresh batteries in them.

    _____ All detectors will be checked once a week by _____.

ATA 2821 © 1993 American Teaching Aids • Minneapolis, MN • Made in U.S.A.

Fire Safety Game

Make a matching game to play with someone else. Glue the sheet to a piece of construction paper. Color the cards and cut them out. Place cards upside down in a square. Take turns turning up two cards at a time. If you find a match, keep it and take another turn. Read what your match says as you pick it up, and follow any additional directions on the card. If you miss, let the next person have a turn. Continue until all cards are matched.

Junior Volunteer Fire Fighter

At the end of the unit, give each child a certificate, signed by the teacher or a local fire fighter, as well as a badge to color and wear.

THIS IS TO CERTIFY THAT

_____

is a

JUNIOR VOLUNTEER FIRE FIGHTER
of the

_____Fire Department.

_____ has learned how to prevent the start of fires and how

to get away from them safely.

Signed _____   Title_____

Date _____

Official Junior Fire Fighter Badge

ATA 2821 © 1993 American Teaching Aids • Minneapolis, MN • Made in U.S.A.

Good Books for Your "Fire Station" Corner

Elliot, Dan. *A Visit to the Sesame Street Firehouse.*
New York: Random House, 1983.
Provides an overview of the different kinds of equipment used to fight a variety of fires.

Gibbons, Gail. *Fire! Fire!*
New York: Thomas Y. Crowell, 1984.
Shows various ways in which fires are fought.

Kunhardt, Edith. *I Want To Be a Fire Fighter.*
New York: Grosset & Dunlap, 1989.
A girl talks about her father's work as a volunteer fire fighter.

Maass, Robert. *Fire Fighters.*
New York: Scholastic, 1989.
Provides a behind-the-scenes look at the life of a big-city fire fighter.

Marston, Hope Irvin. *Fire Trucks.*
Spring Valley, N.Y.: Dodd, Mead & Co., 1984.
Comprehensive look at different kinds of fire-fighting equipment.

Rey, Margaret and Shalleck, Allan J. *Curious George at the Fire Station.*
Boston: Houghton Mifflin, 1985.
Curious George sets off a false alarm while visiting the fire station but redeems himself by rescuing a Dalmation puppy.

Rockwell, Anne F. *Fire Engines.*
New York: Dutton, 1986.
Describes parts of a fire engine and tells how they are used to fight fires.

ATA 2821 © 1993 American Teaching Aids • Minneapolis, MN • Made in U.S.A.